Off the Beaten Path
Calendar 2021

18 Months
October 2020 through March 2022

2021

January

S	M	T	W	Th	F	Sa
					1	2
3	4	5	6	7	8	9
10	11	12	13	14	15	16
17	18	19	20	21	22	23
24	25	26	27	28	29	30
31						

February

S	M	T	W	Th	F	Sa
	1	2	3	4	5	6
7	8	9	10	11	12	13
14	15	16	17	18	19	20
21	22	23	24	25	26	27
28						

March

S	M	T	W	Th	F	Sa
	1	2	3	4	5	6
7	8	9	10	11	12	13
14	15	16	17	18	19	20
21	22	23	24	25	26	27
28	29	30	31			

April

S	M	T	W	Th	F	Sa
				1	2	3
4	5	6	7	8	9	10
11	12	13	14	15	16	17
18	19	20	21	22	23	24
25	26	27	28	29	30	

May

S	M	T	W	Th	F	Sa
						1
2	3	4	5	6	7	8
9	10	11	12	13	14	15
16	17	18	19	20	21	22
23	24	25	26	27	28	29
30	31					

June

S	M	T	W	Th	F	Sa
		1	2	3	4	5
6	7	8	9	10	11	12
13	14	15	16	17	18	19
20	21	22	23	24	25	26
27	28	29	30			

July

S	M	T	W	Th	F	Sa
				1	2	3
4	5	6	7	8	9	10
11	12	13	14	15	16	17
18	19	20	21	22	23	24
25	26	27	28	29	30	31

August

S	M	T	W	Th	F	Sa
1	2	3	4	5	6	7
8	9	10	11	12	13	14
15	16	17	18	19	20	21
22	23	24	25	26	27	28
29	30	31				

September

S	M	T	W	Th	F	Sa
			1	2	3	4
5	6	7	8	9	10	11
12	13	14	15	16	17	18
19	20	21	22	23	24	25
26	27	28	29	30		

October

S	M	T	W	Th	F	Sa
					1	2
3	4	5	6	7	8	9
10	11	12	13	14	15	16
17	18	19	20	21	22	23
24	25	26	27	28	29	30
31						

November

S	M	T	W	Th	F	Sa
	1	2	3	4	5	6
7	8	9	10	11	12	13
14	15	16	17	18	19	20
21	22	23	24	25	26	27
28	29	30				

December

S	M	T	W	Th	F	Sa
			1	2	3	4
5	6	7	8	9	10	11
12	13	14	15	16	17	18
19	20	21	22	23	24	25
26	27	28	29	30	31	

Toronto, Canada: Image by Scott Webb from Pixabay
Toronto City Hall

October 2020

Sunday	Monday	Tuesday	Wednesday	Thursday	Friday	Saturday
				1	2	3
4	5  Child Health Day	6	7	8	9	10
11	12  Columbus Day	13	14	15	16	17
18	19	20	21	22	23	24
25	26	27	28	29	30	31  Halloween

Osaka, Japan: Sumiyoshi Taisha Grand Shrine
By Saigen Jiro - Own work, CC0, https://commons.wikimedia.org/w/index.php?curid=61833735

November 2020

Sunday	Monday	Tuesday	Wednesday	Thursday	Friday	Saturday
1  Daylight Saving Time Ends	2	3 	4	5	6	7
8	9	10	11 	12	13	14
15	16	17	18	19	20	21
22	23	24	25	26 	27 It's Black Friday 	28
29	30 					

Pokhara, Nepal 2: View of Phewa lake and Pokhara from Shanti Stupa
By Dhruba Gajurel - Own work, CC BY-SA 3.0, https://commons.wikimedia.org/w/index.php?curid=33076674

December 2020

Sunday	Monday	Tuesday	Wednesday	Thursday	Friday	Saturday
		1	2	3	4	5
6	7  Pearl Harbor Day	8	9	10	11	12
13	14	15	16	17	18	19
20	21  Winter Solstice	22	23	24  Christmas Eve	25  Christmas Day	26
27	28	29	30	31 New Year's Eve 		

Copenhagen, Denmark: Image by Rolands Varsbergs from Pixabay
https://cdn.pixabay.com/photo/2019/03/13/11/04/copenhagen-4052654_960_720.jpg

January 2021

Sunday	Monday	Tuesday	Wednesday	Thursday	Friday	Saturday
					1 	2
3	4	5	6	7	8	9
10	11	12	13	14	15	16
17	18  MLK Day	19	20	21	22	23
24	25	26	27	28	29	30
31						

White River, Arkansas-Missouri
By Linda Tanner (flickr user: goingslo) - https://www.flickr.com/photos/goingslo/2229876591/, CC BY 2.0, https://commons.wikimedia.org/w/index.php?curid=23210086

February 2021

Sunday	Monday	Tuesday	Wednesday	Thursday	Friday	Saturday
	1 	2 	3	4	5	6
7	8	9	10	11	12  Chinese New Year	13
14  Valentine's Day	15 	16 	17	18	19	20
21	22	23	24	25	26	27
28						

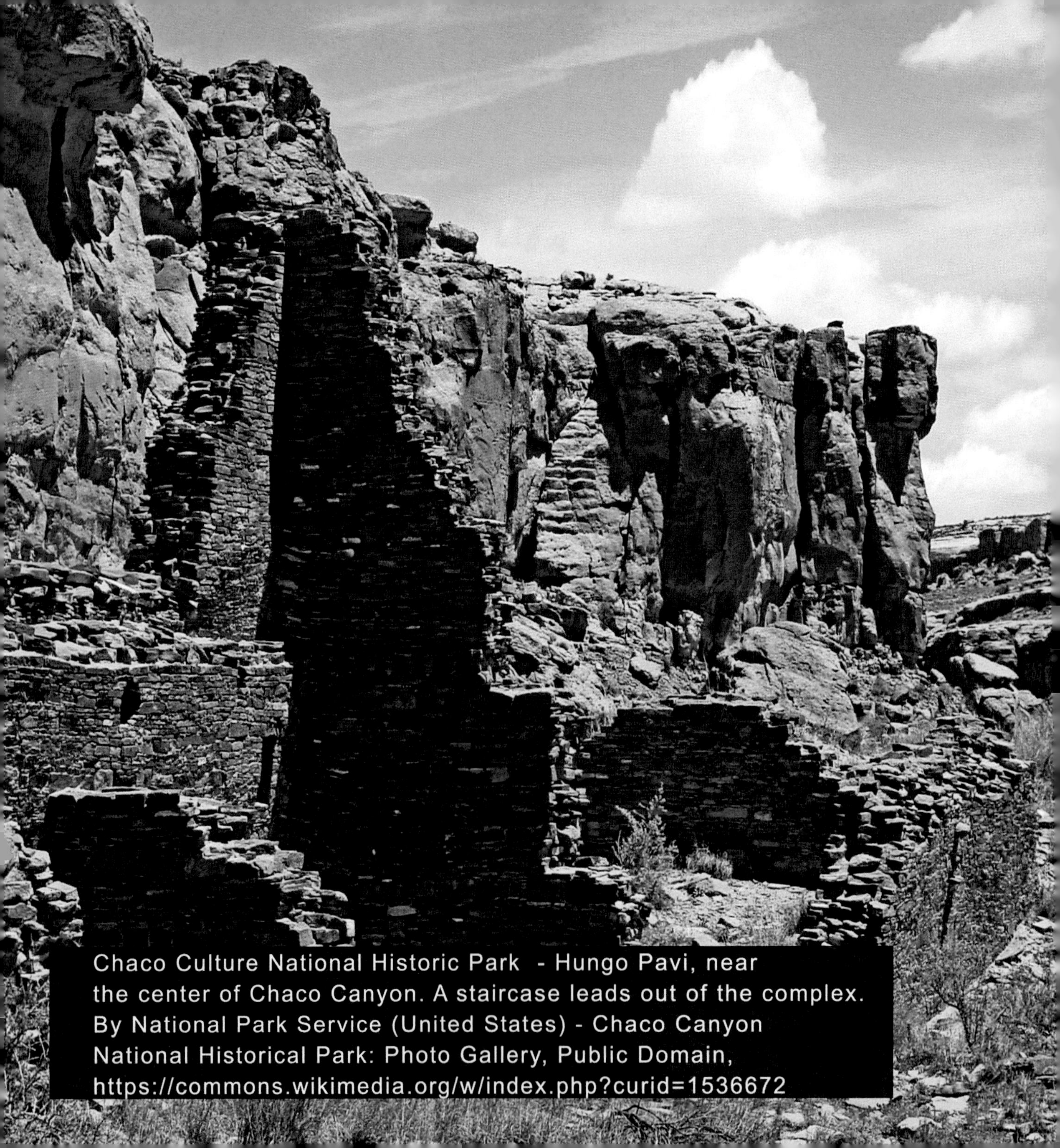

Chaco Culture National Historic Park - Hungo Pavi, near the center of Chaco Canyon. A staircase leads out of the complex. By National Park Service (United States) - Chaco Canyon National Historical Park: Photo Gallery, Public Domain, https://commons.wikimedia.org/w/index.php?curid=1536672

March 2021

Sunday	Monday	Tuesday	Wednesday	Thursday	Friday	Saturday
	1	2	3	4	5	6
7	8	9	10	11	12	13
14  Daylight Saving Time Begins	15	16	17 	18	19	20 
21	22	23	24	25	26	27
28	29 	30	31			

Ventura, USA
By Ken Lund - https://www.flickr.com/photos/kenlund/4083986408/, CC BY-SA 2.0, https://commons.wikimedia.org/w/index.php?curid=16430661

April 2021

Sunday	Monday	Tuesday	Wednesday	Thursday	Friday	Saturday
				1	2	3
4  Easter Sunday	5	6	7	8	9	10
11	12	13	14	15 	16	17
18	19	20	21	22	23	24
25	26	27	28	29	30	

Acadia National Park, Maine.
Image by nsmeinzer from Pixabay

May 2021

Sunday	Monday	Tuesday	Wednesday	Thursday	Friday	Saturday
						1
2	3	4	5 	6 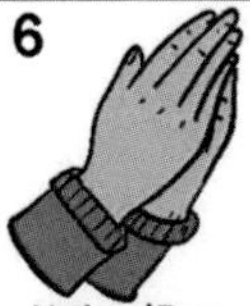 National Day of Prayer	7	8
9 	10	11	12	13	14	15 
16	17	18	19	20	21  Defense Transportation Day	22
23	24	25	26	27	28	29
30	31 					

Tarpon Springs, FL: Sponge docks.

June 2021

Sunday	Monday	Tuesday	Wednesday	Thursday	Friday	Saturday
		1	2	3	4	5
6	7	8	9	10	11	12
13	14  Flag Day	15	16	17	18	19
20 	21	22	23	24	25	26
27	28	29	30			

Launceston, Australia: Aerial perspective of Cataract Gorge and its surrounds with the Tamar River
By Bob T - Own work, CC BY-SA 4.0, https://commons.wikimedia.org/w/index.php?curid=69706659

July 2021

Sunday	*Monday*	*Tuesday*	*Wednesday*	*Thursday*	*Friday*	*Saturday*
				1	2	3
4 	5	6	7	8	9	10
11	12	13	14	15	16	17
18	19	20	21	22	23	24
25  Parents Day	26	27	28	29	30	31

Channel Islands National Park - Santa Cruz Island in the spring.
By Albertdom - Own work, CC BY-SA 4.0, https://commons.wikimedia.org/w/index.php?curid=52734499

August 2021

Sunday	Monday	Tuesday	Wednesday	Thursday	Friday	Saturday
1	2	3	4	5	6	7  Purple Heart Day
8	9	10	11	12	13	14
15	16	17	18	19  Aviation Day	20	21
22	23	24	25	26	27	28
29	30	31				

Mumbai, India: Chhatrapati Shivaji Maharaj Terminus at night
By Deepak Deshmukh - Own work, CC BY-SA 4.0, https://commons.wikimedia.org/w/index.php?curid=62829752

September 2021

Sunday	Monday	Tuesday	Wednesday	Thursday	Friday	Saturday
			1	2	3	4
5	6 	7	8	9	10	11 
12  Grandparents' Day	13	14	15	16	17  Citizenship Day	18
19	20	21	22  Fall Begins	23	24	25
26	27	28	29	30		

Sarasota, Florida - Marie Selby Botanical Gardens
By SibylRose - Own work, CC BY-SA 3.0,
https://commons.wikimedia.org/w/index.php?curid=35462387

October 2021

Sunday	Monday	Tuesday	Wednesday	Thursday	Friday	Saturday
					1	2
3	4 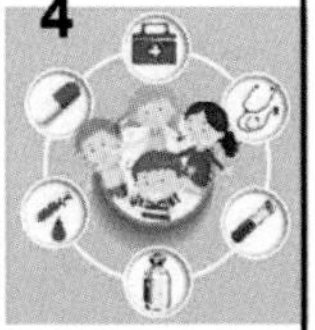 Child Health Day	5	6	7	8	9
10	11 	12	13	14	15 	16
17	18	19	20	21	22	23
24	25	26	27	28	29	30
31  Hallowe'en						

November 2021

Sunday	*Monday*	*Tuesday*	*Wednesday*	*Thursday*	*Friday*	*Saturday*
	1	2 	3	4	5	6
7  Daylight Saving Time Ends	8	9	10	11 	12	13
14	15	16	17	18	19	20
21	22	23	24	25 	26 	27
28	29 	30				

Image by Denis Doukhan from Pixabay
Shopping center in Bristol, England

December 2021

Sunday	Monday	Tuesday	Wednesday	Thursday	Friday	Saturday
			1	2	3	4
5	6	7  Pearl Harbor Day	8	9	10	11
12	13	14	15	16	17	18
19	20  Winter Arrives	21	22	23	24  Christmas Eve	25 
26	27	28	29	30	31  New Year's Eve	

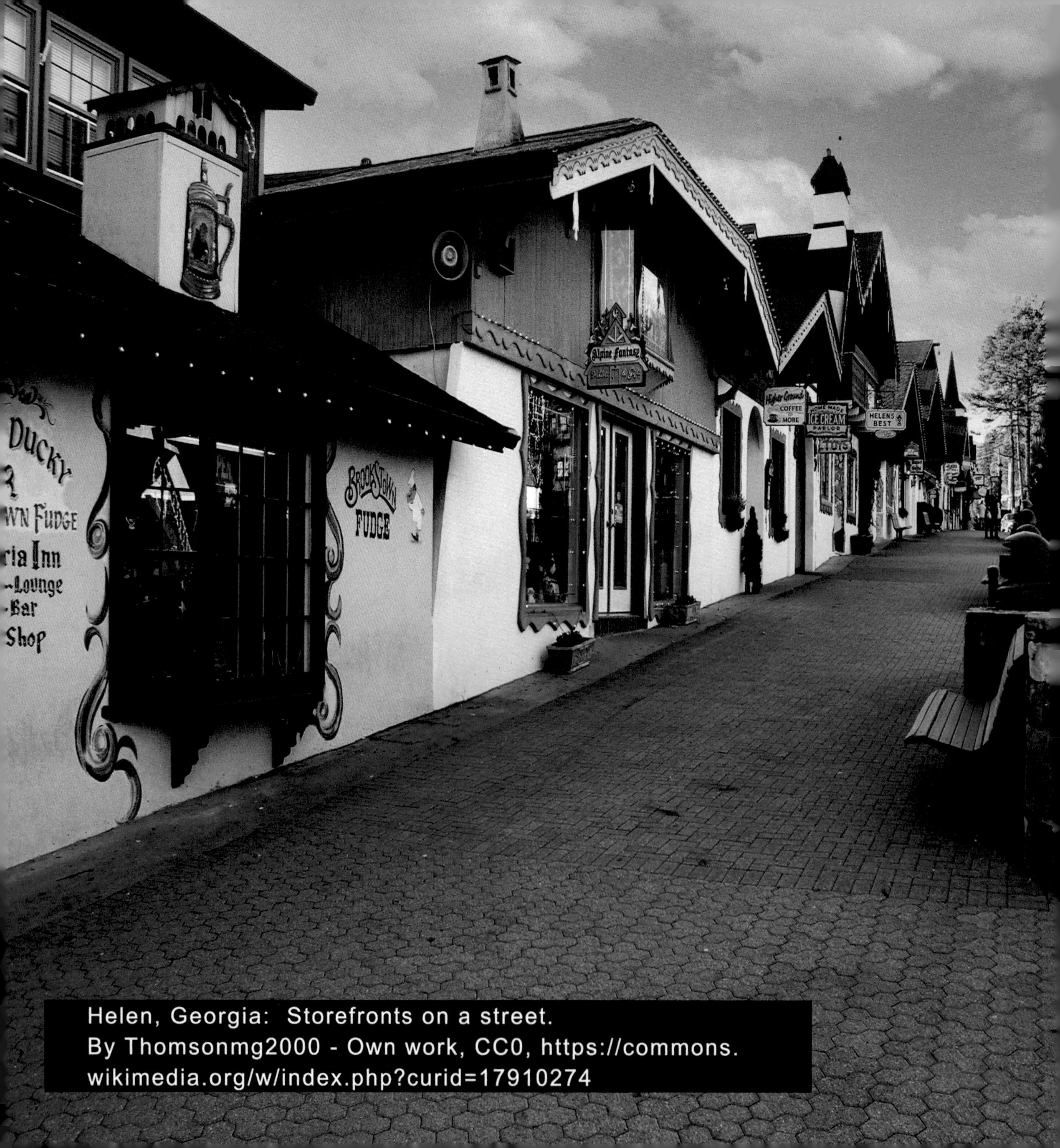

Helen, Georgia: Storefronts on a street.
By Thomsonmg2000 - Own work, CC0, https://commons.wikimedia.org/w/index.php?curid=17910274

January 2022

Sunday	Monday	Tuesday	Wednesday	Thursday	Friday	Saturday
						1 
2	3	4	5	6	7	8
9	10	11	12	13	14	15
16	17 	18	19	20	21	22
23	24	25	26	27	28	29
30	31					

Phewa Lake, Pokhara, Nepal

February 2022

Sunday	Monday	Tuesday	Wednesday	Thursday	Friday	Saturday
		1  Chinese New Year	2 	3	4	5
6	7	8	9	10	11	12
13	14 	15	16	17	18	19
20	21 	22	23	24	25	26
27	28					

Rio de Janiero, Brazil: Bondinho do Pão de Açúcar, Rio de Janeiro, Brazil
Photo by Davi Costa on Unsplash